Messengers

DIVINE ENCOUNTERS

Deacon John and Mary Scott

ISBN 979-8-88832-902-3 (paperback)
ISBN 979-8-88832-903-0 (digital)

Christian Faith Publishing
832 Park Avenue
Meadville, PA 16335
www.christianfaithpublishing.com

Printed in the United States of America

We lovingly dedicate this book to our
children and grandchildren.

Contents

Introduction

One of my pastors told my wife and me that many of our Divine encounters are not *coincidences* but *Christ-incidences*. We came to know more what he meant as our years rolled by. These encounters are symbolized in our story by the men who just seem to *show up* at Father Bernard's parish. We call them God's messengers. Others call them angels. We have found out through the years that you have to be awake to recognize these messengers and absorb God's guidance.

In the Catholic Church, we encounter God (Christ) in the Word (scriptures), especially in the Eucharist (Holy Communion) and in the seven sacraments: Baptism, Holy Communion, Confirmation, Confession (Penance), Marriage (Matrimony), Holy Orders, and Anointing of the Sick. At these specific times, the Church teaches that Jesus is present with us! We explain to our parishioners that this is when Jesus "rubs shoulders with us," a real, physical presence of the Divine.

But we believe we more frequently encounter the Divine in other places and ways, usually outside the Church and through others. This story is one of those *ways*, when the Divine sends us *messengers*, fellow believers, to help us along our journey. These messengers can appear suddenly in our lives when we least expect them but surely need them. We may not know them or ever see them again except for that brief encounter. You see, God isn't distant, as in the song "From a Distance," but He's closer than we think, loves us more than we know, and watches out for us, through thick and thin. It's hard to have this faith during the *thick* times, the hard lessons of life—deaths, sickness, pandemics, etc.—but He's there for us. That's the message of this story. God is real, not distant. He is present, near, and with and in us, and He wants the best for us.

We chose to make the crucifix (Jesus crucified) a focus, the centerpiece of this story because it is on the cross where God fully revealed (and reveals) His great love for us.

We take full responsibility for all errors of liturgy or Church teachings in this story, but as in our real lives, which are full of errors and aren't always exact, this story attempts to focus on the most important thing in our lives—we are not alone!

We hope you enjoy this story and it gives you pause to think and evaluate your own faith journey. We wrote it mainly for our children and grandchildren so that they will feel the love of Christ in their lives and never be afraid. Christ has been there for us through some rough times, and we believe He will be there for you. Just remember to answer the door when He knocks.

The Janitor's Discovery

You also must be prepared, for at an hour you
do not expect, the Son of Man will come.

—Luke 12:40

It was the janitor who first noticed He was missing. Sweeping and dusting, washing the old oaken floors, and polishing the pews was an all-day job for Joe, the custodian of St. Thomas's parish in Jasper, Missouri. He always started early on Monday morning, before the weekday Mass, sweeping out between the pews and then buffing and shinning the scarred and dented wood with lemon-oil polish. It was his favorite time to work, as the church was empty, and the sun was just coming up. The rays of the sun shone through the stained glass of the large circular window behind the altar in a dazzling display of color.

Today, he noticed a lingering smell of incense from last Sunday's Mass and a peaceful stillness in the building. Old memories usually flooded in as Joe lovingly began his routine. St. Thomas had about fifty old wooden pews, handmade as the church was built, probably in the late 1880s. Joe loved to run his hands over their polished surfaces, smelling the sweet scent of the oil, and seeing the sun reflected off the sheen of the old oaken seats.

He had been raised in those pews, sitting in the second row, on the left side of the church, sandwiched between his mom, his dad, and his two brothers and younger sister, who could never sit still. His deceased parents had been deeply devoted and supportive members of the parish. St. Thomas had been serving generations of farmers and hardworking families. Smiling, he recalled all the sacraments he had received in this beautiful old church, especially when he and his beloved Cathy received the sacrament of marriage.

The church had a *solid* look, as it was built with large blocks of stone and hand-cut wooden beams. The stones had come from a quarry about a hundred miles to the south and were then transported by oxen-drawn wagons. The wood was from the forests to the north of town. Once he read that it took two years to build the church, with most of the skilled laborers coming from the local farms and factories. They had even imported some master builders from Europe, and their input was invaluable. The town had pitched in and put not only their capital but their sweat equity into the construction of the church.

Joe, who was skilled with his hands, admired those early craftsmen who built the church. He especially was in awe of the unknown person who carved the crucifix. At times, the figure of Jesus on the cross seemed to be revealing a message to him.

The church was designed on a simple plan in the shape of a cross, one which had been used all across the Western states as the faith spread out from the Eastern Seaboard. It was one of the most imposing buildings in the town, and it stood out with its carved facade and large wooden doors reminding many of the European churches. Indeed, that's most likely where the design originated.

Large oak trees lined the street running in front of the church, and there was a well-used children's park on the northern side. On the southern side was an old parish cemetery, with its moss-laden headstones and rusty iron railings. Statues of angels and Celtic crosses filled the old graveyard. Family names from years past brought memories back to those who still lived in Jasper.

St. Thomas the Apostle Parish gave one a feeling of permanence, of something that would last through the years surviving all the wars, epidemics, and social unrest. Joe remembered the remodeling done after the Vatican II Council when the carved, wooden altar was turned around to face the *flock* as the priest said prayers and consecrated the hosts, and the old wooden prayer rail had been removed. The church altar was on its eastern end. It was placed under the apse, the point where the east and west transepts were crossed by the northern-southern galleries. The idea was that the morning sun would shine through the stained glass on the priest as he began the Mass. Most mornings, Joe spent a few moments reflecting in front of the simply carved statues of the Holy Mary and St. Joseph carrying the infant Jesus.

There were a lot of changes in the last years, as the liturgy of the Holy Mass had been rewritten to allow more participation by the parish families. Since Vatican II, only a few responses in the liturgy were in Latin. Even more contemporary church music was now a prominent part of the service. It had taken Joe a couple of years to get used to the new changes, but now he enjoyed the Mass even more, especially the music. Pausing a moment, he fondly remembered that his sweet wife, Cathy, had a beautiful voice and enjoyed singing in the parish choir. She was also a dedicated volunteer at the parish food bank. Cathy had often reminded Joe that their special prayer was to help each other get to heaven.

Five years ago, his beloved Cathy was buried in the parish graveyard. This church had once been an important part of his family life. But since Cathy's death from cancer, he was now the only family member remaining in the town. Although each Sunday, he still sat in the same pew, listening to the latest in a succession of priests who were assigned as pastors to the parish, it just didn't have the same old, homey feeling of belonging.

Joe hadn't lost his faith, though he almost had after Cathy's passing. Cathy once told him that her suffering had brought her closer to Jesus on the cross. It had been hard for him to accept her suffering and death, yet he had remained in the parish. It was the friendship and ministering of his late friend and pastor, Father Richard Jones, who counseled him and actually helped strengthen his faith. Like Joe, Fr. Richard had served in the Vietnam War and understood and shared his struggles, doubts, and disabilities. They both had been wounded, especially Joe, who still had shrapnel in his right leg and walked with a slight limp. Fr. Richard had helped Joe realize that there's no sin or struggle greater than God's mercy. Joe now felt at ease with the Church and his faith. It was just that so much had recently changed in the parish that he thought perhaps a change of scenery might be good for him.

The number of parishioners had slowly dwindled in the last ten years or so, especially after the priest scandals. One of the parish priests had been removed and reassigned due to complaints and accusations from the parishioners. That was when Father Richard had been brought in, and he was a breath of fresh air for the parish. After Father Richard died a few years back, at least twenty to thirty of the parishioners had simply stopped coming to church. Joe heard from some that they were just mad at the Catholic Church and fed up with the seemingly never-ending reports of abuse and mismanagement. Now seeing an influx of new, younger families coming into town was encouraging. Perhaps the Holy Spirit would bring a new awakening and more folks to Mass.

Joe had started even earlier this quiet Monday morning, a full hour before the usual time. He always began after he had his first cup of coffee from the back sacristy's new coffeemaker, enjoying that cup of coffee as he sat in the overstuffed, leather chair. His mind often wandered back into the past. He could still imagine his humble friend, Father Richard, sitting there with him, talking about Bishop Downes's latest ideas, if the Cardinals had won, and how many homers Albert Pujols had hit. The new and current pastor, Father Bernard, much younger than Joe, didn't seem to want to establish or cultivate a relationship that Joe had with some of the other pastors. There was an aloofness and restlessness about him that separated him from others. And this priest especially didn't like baseball.

Today things were becoming more businesslike. It wasn't the same friendly, old parish of his family. Joe thought more and more about retiring and starting a fishing camp, maybe up at Lake Hansen twenty miles away. Or maybe he'd move to Texas where his younger brother lived. He had even considered a pilgrimage to Spain called the Camino de Santiago. After all, he thought, *What was I waiting for? What was I hoping for?* As long as he could take Sam (his loyal black Labrador service dog), he would be comfortable anywhere. Sam was always helping him navigate in the church and around town. Joe smiled as he looked at Sam sitting in the aisle, seemingly looking up at the altar and the cross.

He was about halfway through the rows of pews when he thought he heard a muffled moan, then a sound as if someone or something had fallen or landed on the sanctuary's floor. Sam raised his head and turned toward the rear of the church. Looking up, Joe saw nothing and continued his work. In years past, there had been *critters* coming into the church at night trying to keep warm from the cold, windy Missouri winter. Joe took pains to always make sure all the doors and windows were closed and locked, but somehow animals would sneak into the building. One time, he'd even found a fox and her kit lying up near the altar, right under the cross. It was becoming warmer in the sanctuary as the sun rose higher in the east. Joe thought to himself that perhaps he'd heard an outside thump, from some truck on the nearby main road, or a passing crow landing on the windowsill. He paid no more attention to it and continued on down the pew; his routine was practiced and measured after more than twenty years of service to the parish.

Minutes later, as the sun continued to rise illuminating the entire sanctuary and altar, his eyes moved to the large crucifix hanging above the center of the sanctuary. The intense glare from the sun's reflection made it hard to see, but shading his eyes with his left hand, he gazed at the cross. Suddenly Joe dropped his broom and rags.

He couldn't believe his eyes! Where was the figure of Jesus, which had been hanging on the cross just last night when he locked the church up? It simply was not there! Confused, he removed and cleaned his glasses and looked upward. Nope, it wasn't there. He knew it had been there; at least he thought so. Besides, how could a life-size wooden figure of Jesus Christ just vanish? Sitting down, Joe tried to focus on what he was seeing, or more importantly, not seeing.

Yup, the figure of Christ was missing, and it hadn't just fallen off the cross. It wasn't there on the floor at all. His mind raced through the possibilities. Had someone stolen the wooden figure last night, and who would do such a thing, and why? Had it been taken down earlier in the morning for some maintenance, or refinishing, and no one had told him? Father Bernard did have a habit of making decisions and not sharing what was happening. The cross suspended above the altar was moving slowly to the currents of the church's forced air heating system, which Joe had turned on as he entered the building earlier that morning. Scratching his head, he wondered what was going on!

It was then that Joe had a strange sensation that he was not alone in the church. It wasn't a chill that came over him, more of a warmness. But he surely felt something or someone's presence was there with him. As he turned toward the rear of the church, his eyes sought out the corners and nooks of the old building, and he squinted hard to see if someone had come into the church as he was working. Yet it seemed empty. Looking back at the cross every couple of seconds, he got up and walked back down the center aisle toward the front door of the church, toward the small narthex. Hesitantly opening the door, he checked the area for an early parishioner or an animal. Nothing moved in the tranquil quiet of the illuminated building, as it creaked, warming from the sun's rays.

Satisfied that no one had apparently come into the church, Joe reentered, and moving slowly across the rear of the church, he noticed that one of the doors to a large, antique confessional was partially open. It was one of those ancient works of wood that had elaborate carving, and it looked like a large closet. Many folks didn't use them anymore. They preferred to confess when they even did approach the Sacrament, with a face-to-face encounter with the priest rather than with the shadowy privacy screen of the confessional separating them.

Opening the door of the old confessional, Joe was startled to see the body of a young man crumpled up on the seat, apparently sound asleep. The man's wrinkled, unkept clothes indicated that he was homeless. He apparently was one of those drifters who had seemingly taken over the town's park in the summer and then dispersed to warm sleeping places in the winter. His stained, dirty backpack and wooden staff leaned against the confessional's walls.

The parish had trouble in the near past with these guys and sometimes gals, but new signs and locked doors had recently kept the undesirables out of the church. The parish council and the pastor had made it clear to Joe that security was one of the highest priorities. They wouldn't be happy to learn that someone was sleeping in *their* church and especially hiding in the confessional. As Joe further opened the door the man fell, his long legs spilling out onto the floor. Old leather shoes and work gloves went with his tattered winter coat. Yup, he was a homeless guy alright, and Joe had interrupted what was a deep, warm sleep.

Casting a quick glance over his shoulder to the empty cross, Joe began to rouse the man from his slumber. As the slim stranger stood, it was apparent that he was over six feet, almost a half-foot taller than Joe. There was dust on the man's shoes, and Joe wondered where he picked up dust in the recent wet weather. "What are you doing in my church?" Joe said, rather forcefully. "And, where did you come from?" Before the man could answer, Joe was quickly grabbing his dirty rucksack and wooden staff and pushing them into the man's hands, at the same time guiding him toward the church's front door. "Don't you know this is private property, and not open to vagrants like you?" he blurted out to the man. "This is God's house. You can't just come in here and sleep as if it were your home or something!"

"I'm sorry, sir," said the stranger. "I just needed a place to warm up and spend the night. I don't have any money, and nobody would give me a room or cot. The shelters were all filled. The church was the last place I could turn to." As Joe sized the man up, he could tell that he had probably been on the road awhile. Most likely he was traveling from town to town, sleeping where he could, and where possibly someone would take him in and feed him. "Well, you can't stay here," Joe sternly said. "This is a church, and nobody can just walk in or out as they please. We keep this place closed and locked up at night. Security is important. We have a lot of valuable stuff here and must protect it."

The stranger looked intently at him and nodded, indicating he understood. "Sorry to have made trouble for you, Brother," the stranger calmly said. It was then that Joe saw the eyes. As he looked into the stranger's gentle eyes, he seemed to get lost in them, lost in the same warmness he had felt earlier.

The stranger seemed to look into him, not at him. But there was a softness to the stranger's gaze, and a warm smile went along with a humble demeanor. Joe even noticed old Sam's wagging tail and unusual interest in this fellow. He decided right then that this stranger posed no harm to himself or the church. As the stranger began to leave, Joe paused and asked, "Like a cup of coffee, buddy?" The man immediately stopped and turned around, and that broad smile came back over his face. "Sure, that would be great," he said. Joe motioned to him to follow him into the back sacristy where the coffee aroma filled the room. Leaving his backpack outside the door but holding on to his wooden staff, the young stranger entered. "Have a seat. My name is Joe. What's yours? And what are you doing roaming around our town during the winter?"

"My name is Raphael," the stranger said as he eased himself into the overstuffed chair.

Smiling, the stranger took the nicked white coffee mug and swirling the warm cup between his fingers answered, "I'm looking for a friend of mine, who may be lost." Still curious, Joe asked, "So you are just traveling around this part of the country in the snow, looking for a lost friend?"

"Yes, that's about the size of it," said the stranger, taking a long, deep draught of the steaming coffee. "This stuff is sure good. Hits the spot."

It was then that Joe remembered the empty cross in the church. Troubled, he wondered what he would say to the new pastor who would be coming in at any minute for morning Mass. How would he explain the empty crucifix and the presence of this vagrant in the sacristy? Things were becoming complicated in a very short time.

"You wouldn't perhaps know anything about our crucifix hanging above the altar, would you?" Joe asked. "We seem to be missing the figure of Jesus who hung on the cross, and I don't know where to find Him. Know anything about this?"

Raphael, leaning to the right and peering through the open sacristy door, looked up at the cross, smiled, and shook his head. "Yup, it's empty all right, and Jesus surely isn't there."

....

Chapter 2

The Pastor's Response

It was not you who chose me, but I who chose you and appointed you to go and bear fruit that will remain, so that whatever you ask the Father in my name he may give you.

—John 15:16

The young pastor Fr. Bernard got up that morning with the same daily routine he always followed since coming to St. Thomas the Apostle Parish a year and a half ago. Making the sign of the cross, he began his morning prayers. He showered, shaved, and combed back his short dark hair. Each morning, he drank only one cup of coffee with no sugar or cream as usual. He then checked the notes on his desk to see if there were any emergencies he'd have to deal with that morning. Pulling his heavy coat over his cassock, he adjusted his cap (one of those most popular with young priests, which looked flat with a small brim). Going over to the mirror, he checked his polished appearance and half smiled at his crisp black clerics, which were not as faded or tattered as some of the older priests, who seemed to disregard their appearance. He then went out the front door of the rectory, locked it, and began the short walk over to the church for Mass, leaving his own deep footprints in the newly fallen snow. Over to his left was the parish graveyard with its odd collection of headstones and crosses, some in disrepair and some brand new. The newly fallen snow made strange *caps* on the headstones. For a few seconds, he stopped to try and discern what shapes they were in.

He hadn't experienced much snow in his life, especially during his childhood in Alabama. His beloved grandfather, Gene, lived close to him and had first introduced him to the Catholic faith. Granddad made sure he got to weekly Mass, even when his parents were too busy with work. Snow in Alabama was rare, as were Catholics in that part of the country.

Fondly, he remembered the beautiful spring days of blooming pink azaleas and dogwood trees. Their promises of the Easter season always reminded him of new life and hope. Missing his family and friends who lived so far away, he promised himself he would soon visit them.

Last night, he awoke hearing noises, which he thought came from the church itself. He had even walked over to the darkened church and let himself in the back door to the sacristy. Checking the building for signs of entry, he was satisfied that nothing seemed out of place. Once again he glanced up and saw the figure of Jesus on the crucifix and reminded himself to get with Joseph, the janitor. They needed to have the statue cleaned before Easter. Returning to the rectory, he plopped back into bed for what he hoped would be a deep sleep.

Father Bernard hadn't been sleeping soundly for weeks. Some nights he stayed awake, ruminating over his vocation. He wondered what he was doing here in this small parish and what his future held. He felt lonely and that something was missing in his life. In his prior assignment, he had been the vicar of a larger parish, near a university. The atmosphere was one of the academic conversations and stimulating friendships, and the parish was full of young people and *life*. He constantly wondered why the bishop had sent him out here to a small, struggling, more working-class congregation, now suffering from meager weekly contributions from its dwindling parishioners. Already he had been forced to let the director of religious education go.

It seemed as if more separations might be unavoidable in the near future unless finances improved.

Father Bernard had hoped to be assigned to an academic post at the nearby seminary or as a professor of theology. After all, he had his PhD from the Catholic University. Discouraged, he had begun to question why he had been called to become a priest. It was all becoming a little too consuming, and he felt as if he had nobody to talk with. Even his parents did not support his priestly vocation. He felt alone and conflicted, praying that God would tell him what to do.

Reaching for the large wooden door, he kicked the snow off his boots. To his surprise, he found the church locked. Concerned, he wondered why the janitor Joseph (Father preferred to be more formal with his parish employees) had not unlocked it earlier. After all, there were those particular parishioners who usually came by the church early every morning, to pray before hurrying off for work or taking their kids to school. If they found the door locked, he'd hear about it soon.

After glancing at the crucifix, Father again reminded himself of the needed cleaning, then headed back toward the back sacristy. He could already smell the coffee and hear Joseph's voice talking to someone. Father wondered who would be in the sacristy with Joseph this early in the morning. He had warned Joseph to try and keep lay people out of the sacristy, as it was reserved for priests and ministers to vest before Mass and definitely wasn't meant to be a meeting place for parishioners.

It's not that I'm a hard man, Father Bernard thought to himself as he weaved through the pews, *but one does have to be particular with God's church, and its sacred furnishings, which I am entrusted with.* Not just anybody should be allowed to roam freely within the church.

As he neared the sacristy, Joseph came out of the doorway and almost ran into him. "Oh, good morning, Father…," Joe stammered. "Didn't expect you over so soon." Sam, who was with Joe, brushed against Father and left a trail of dog hair on Father's black clerics.

As usual, Joseph was dressed in tattered jeans, a worn flannel shirt, and old work boots. Dismayed, the priest had been meaning to talk to him about trying to dress more appropriately, as he was concerned about the impression made on his parishioners and visitors. *Can't have church employees not meeting standards, could we?* He put that thought away for future reference. The number of *thoughts* for future discussions and reference were adding up.

Today, Father thought, *Joseph acted more agitated and excited than usual.* It was then that the Father saw the man sitting in his chair in the sacristy, drinking coffee. Another one of the vagrants Joseph allowed into the church, the priest surmised, a person who needed to be taken down to one of the local soup kitchens for a meal. As Father entered the sacristy, the stranger didn't even stand up. "Good morning, Father," the man grinned, "offer you a cup? It's good, hot, and strong."

"No, thanks," said the pastor as he critically sized up this unexpected visitor. "It's too close to morning Mass. By the way, Joseph, who is our guest?" Joe, looking haggard and sheepish, introduced Father Bernard to Raphael. "So, Raphael, what brings you to our church this early morning?" Father Bernard asked with authority.

Still, the mysterious stranger didn't move from the chair or politely stand. (*A lack of manners and training in church etiquette*, the priest surmised. Father Bernard was used to people standing respectfully when he was being introduced.) Taking a more determined approach, Father Bernard said, "Would you mind if I sat in my chair?" Raphael immediately moved out of the chair. Picking up his staff, he crossed the room and then turned back toward Joe and the pastor. "Nope, not at all, didn't mean to offend." He smiled.

Sensing the tension in the air, Joe finally mustered up the courage to say something. "Father, Raphael here was just stopping by for a cup of coffee. He'll be leaving soon. He's looking for a friend of his and hoped he might find information about him here."

"Oh," said the pastor, secretly relieved that this man was just passing by. "And, who is this friend you are looking for?" Raphael, moving closer to the two men, looked up and said, "I'm looking for a friend I have lost track of, a fellow who is lost and needs to be found."

"Sounds kind of like a wild-goose chase to me!" Father Bernard exclaimed. "Oh, no," replied Raphael, "in fact, I may have found him recently. I just haven't had the chance to spend time with him and help him." The pastor inwardly chuckled and thought, *This guy, who has been wandering around the countryside, is planning on helping someone else who's lost?*

Witnessing this rather stilted exchange, Joe broke the silence. "Father, could I see you outside for a minute? Raphael, we have some church business to discuss. Would you excuse us for a moment? Then, after the Mass, I'll be glad to drive you down to our St. Vincent shelter and get you some hot food and a warm bed."

"Mighty kind of you, Joe," said Raphael. "Thanks for the coffee, Father. It was good to find you… I meant to meet you." The pastor nodded his head and turned to leave the room, curious about Raphael's choice of words—*finding* and *meeting*. Years ago, Father had read somewhere that the name Raphael meant "happy meeting," or something like that.

Outside the sacristy, Joe led his pastor over to the narthex at the front of the church. Turning toward the cross, he pointed upward, "Father, have we done something to the crucifix? I mean, did we take the statue of Jesus down for cleaning or something?" The priest looked up at the familiar wooden carving of Jesus on the cross and was quite perplexed at Joe's question, as nothing seemed different to him. "No, Joseph. Nothing is out of order, except that we do need to clean up the crucifix before Easter so that it is presentable." Joe, shaking his head, suddenly sat down and then knelt on the kneeler in front of him, looking up at the empty cross. "Joseph, are you okay?" asked the pastor, shaking his head and wondering if Joseph was having some sort of an attack.

Chapter 3

The Parishioners Arrive

For where two or three are gathered together in
my name, there am I in the midst of them.

—Matthew 18:20

As usual, the town mayor was one of the first to arrive for morning Mass. He took off his new wool coat in the narthex and hung it in the closet. After pushing open the heavy door to the church, he walked down the aisle. Quickly genuflecting, he took his seat in his usual pew up front. He'd been coming to this church, sitting alone in this same pew, for over thirty years, and now he was moving to a nearby city to accept a higher-paying job. His grown children had all moved away, and he and Sally, his wife, were in the process of a divorce. Sally accused him of being intolerant and unforgiving of others, especially their children. Admittedly, he would miss his respected position in the community, but since being president of the parish council finding enough funds to cover all the church costs was getting too stressful. *It was time to think of himself for a change,* he thought.

A bit on the heavy side, the mayor kneeled and crossed himself as if by habit. He looked up and saw the crucifix swinging slightly in the warm breeze above the heating system. It seemed this morning, as it did most mornings, that the carved face of Jesus on the cross was looking right at him. A little disturbed by this, he sat back in his pew, and opening his missal, he searched to find the readings and prayers for the Mass. Inwardly, he hoped it would be a short Mass, as he had so many tasks on his desk at work. Out of the corner of his eyes, he saw good-natured Joe moving to set the small credence table with the sacramental vessels, the hosts, the ciboria, and the chalice. He watched Joe then straighten the violet fringed altar cloth. Glancing to his right, Mayor Miller saw a stranger sitting near the front, someone he hadn't seen before in the church or around town. The fellow, shabbily dressed, had a full beard and seemed lost in either thought or prayer. The mayor nodded and smiled at him. New folks at morning Mass were seldom seen, and the mayor wanted to make sure he welcomed all visitors or newcomers to his town.

While anxiously waiting for Mass to begin, the mayor heard little Kathleen in the next pew ask her mother why Jesus wasn't on the cross (a little annoyed, he could never understand children's questions, even his own children). Everything to him seemed as usual today on the sanctuary.

Kathleen's attractive young mother, Diane, was deep in prayer. As a single working mother, she worried about how she would be able to afford child care with her new job at the town diner. Her young daughter had been born with her face disfigured by a large birthmark. Diane's husband abandoned them soon after birth, so there was a special bond between Diane and Kathleen. Though many adults and children avoided them, the parish had always made them feel loved. She was especially grateful for Sr. Cecelia and her wise counsel, and she hoped Sister would never leave the parish. Many of the parishioners were at Kathleen's baptism and even had a little reception for her in the hall. Kathleen seemed to love to be with her mother at Mass and especially liked shaking hands with the older people at the sign of peace. Soon it would be Easter, and Diane hoped she would be able to afford a new dress and shoes for Kathleen who loved to dress up.

As the church began to fill with the usual morning parishioners, Joe finished his daily duties. He retired to his usual seat on the left-side pews. Acting as the sacristan, he was also ready to assist the server or the priest as needed, or perhaps serve as a special minister of the Eucharist. Many times, due to the absence of a scheduled lector (reader), he had been pressed into service to read the opening scriptures and Psalm response. Smiling, he reflected on how his Cathy had been a big influence on his transformation to service and prayer. As he nodded to Raphael sitting near, he tried to focus on the Mass just beginning, but now there was yet another stranger sitting quietly. This other fellow he seemed to recognize but couldn't quite place. *It was becoming quite an out-of-ordinary morning*, he thought to himself.

Martha, who was always busy with last-minute tasks, was there. Slipping in just before the start of Mass, she kneeled, crossed herself, and settled into the pew. She smiled hello to her younger sister, Mary Margaret, and to Jim and Max who were the other members of her weekly prayer group. The group had gotten smaller these past years, with the death of Beverly and the moving away of Alfonso. But their weekly time together was precious to all of them and provided a loving forum for sharing and assisting each other through the rough and good times. They had all met at a Cursillo retreat some twelve years ago and remained good friends and prayer partners (daily calling on the Holy Spirit in prayer). Martha felt as if her service in the parish hospitality committee was a special calling. She often wished that Mary Margaret helped more in that committee and not just spend so much of her time at church in prayer and adoration. Yet Martha knew that her own prayers were so often interrupted by distractions, and today she was grateful Mary Margaret had her devotion to prayer, especially with her recent diagnosis.

As Martha opened her daily missal, Mary Margaret leaned over her pew and whispered that apparently, they had taken the figure of Christ off the cross for cleaning. Looking up and confused, Martha didn't understand what her sister was talking about, as the same old, dusty statue of Christ on the cross was there looking right back at her. *Maybe*, Martha thought, *they are going to take the statue down and clean it during the Lenten season.* That's probably what Mary Margaret imagined. Her thin, pale sister seemed today to be struggling and confused with worries. Mary Margaret had been recently diagnosed with stomach cancer, and she was troubled with who would care for her husband, Phil, who had dementia. Martha decided that she would need to spend more time with her sister and support and reassure her. Their faith was strong, and they trusted that Jesus would not abandon their family in this difficult time (just as He had come to the sisters Martha and Mary of Bethany whom they were named after). Grateful that her sister had received the Sacrament of Anointing of the sick, Martha each day prayed for God's healing presence.

Sister Cecilia, wearing her black and white habit, was sitting to the left of the sanctuary, deep in thought. Feeling her older and graying years, she anxiously wondered what was going to happen to her and her vocation. Last week, Father had told her that he was removing her from her role as religious education coordinator and that he would do the job himself. She worried that she would be relegated to a series of meaningless tasks, which was not her reason for coming to St. Thomas some twelve years ago.

Already contacting her Mother Superior in Salt Lake for instructions, Sister Cecilia feared she would be assigned to another state and parish, something that she did not look forward to. *At my age, can I start over in a new parish knowing no one*, she asked herself. She would especially miss teaching the children and preparing them for the sacraments. Guiding the children from their first Holy Communion to the sacrament of Confirmation had filled her soul with deep gratitude and had brought such joy into her life. During sleepless nights, she was having doubts about her future. Saying the Divine Mercy Chaplet of trust and other devotions had become more difficult, yet she knew in her heart that it was important in times of trouble to trust in Jesus and keep praying. She took comfort in what her former priest once told her, "We may not know what tomorrow holds…but we know who holds tomorrow."

Sister saw a new person coming into the church and sitting in the pew near her. He looked vaguely familiar, but she had trouble remembering where she had seen or met him before.

With his full dark beard and a big smile, he looked a lot like those actors she had seen in last night's TV movie, "The King of Kings," an older rendition of Christ's passion. Settling in for the Mass, she knelt and looked up at the crucifix. Sister gasped as she saw that the figure of Christ was absent from the cross! Concerned, she leaned forward. Rubbing her tired eyes and squinting against the light from the morning sun, she stared again. No, the figure of Christ was definitely missing. She'd have to ask Father about it right after Mass. She wondered if he was having it cleaned or painted in preparation for Easter, and no one had told her.

Sister felt a strong but gentle hand on her shoulder and almost jumped from the pew. Turning around, she saw another stranger, a young, tall man, with disheveled blond hair. The mysterious man looked intently at her, apologizing for startling her, and said, "Sister, good to see you this morning. Sorry, I disturbed you. I should have been more reverent in church. I just came into the community and would like to talk with you about the parish and what's happening."

What's happening? she thought irritably. *Well, Jesus isn't up on the Cross. That's what's happening! Where is He?* Collecting herself, she thanked the young man and said she'd see him after Mass. "Raphael," he said his name was. Finally the bells rang, everyone stood, and Father Bernard entered through the side sacristy doors.

The Mass

> May the eyes of your hearts be
> enlightened, that you may know what
> is the hope that belongs to his call.
>
> —Ephesians 1:18

The church was suddenly filled with rays of light, coming through the eastern windows. Today almost twice the usual number of people were present. Wearing his Lenten purple chasuble, Father Bernard genuflected before the tabernacle and moved toward the altar where he reverenced it with a kiss. Moving toward his chair, Father began the Mass with his usual greeting. Looking out, he was somewhat startled when he saw the larger-than-normal crowd. Many of them seemed to be strangers.

It was when the first reading from the Old Testament was to be read that he noticed the lector (the reader) striding toward the ambo was not Mary Margaret but the tall stranger he had met this morning in the sacristy. Surprised, Father almost got up from his chair to stop him but thought better of it and remained seated. The young man, Raphael, reverently bowed before the altar. Then taking his place at the ambo, began to read the Old Testament scripture passage, which was from Jonah. His deep voice carried clearly and succinctly to the rear of the church. He seemed at ease and inspired. Father noticed that the man didn't glance down even once at the Lectionary but seemed to know the scripture reading by heart. There was certainly more to this mysterious fellow than he'd first thought.

Father Bernard suddenly had an intense desire to talk with him more after the Mass. After the reading, Raphael bowed toward the altar and took his seat. The cantor, Miss Smith, then led the parishioners in the Psalm response. As she began the first notes of the "Praise to You, Lord Jesus Christ…"

Father Bernard in a daze, suddenly awoke, remembering he was to read the Gospel, and then deliver the Homily. The Gospel reading this Monday morning was from Luke. As he spoke, it was as if the words of the Gospel and its message flowed through his heart and mind. Beginning his homily, he spoke with clarity and conviction. Parishioners would later call this his best homily ever. It was as if the Holy Spirit was truly speaking through him to the congregation. The Gospel was on faith, signs, and wonders. Finishing with an inspired and uplifting final reflection, "We are to 'see Him' with the eyes of faith," Father took his seat. Father felt grateful and privately wondered how he had been able to deliver such a rousing and heartfelt homily without much preparation. He was shortly to find out how.

Sister Cecelia thought that there were certainly more people than she had lately seen in a usual morning Mass. As she listened to Father's homily, she saw that there were some ten or twelve men, strangers, in the church. Some were sitting together, others alone, but all were very attentive to the liturgy. They all seemed to be simply dressed, and many had full beards. She wondered if there was some meeting locally of a club or something and that these men had come to Mass together. She took another look at the cross, just to assure herself that the wooden statue of Jesus was still not there. The wooden cross remained bare to her eyes. She wasn't imagining it, yet she wondered what God was telling her on the empty cross.

Father, reflecting on his homily, finally stood up to read the Prayers of the Faithful, which always included the parishioners who were sick and homebound. Then he began to set up the altar with the help of the server. Wait! It seemed as if a new server had appeared and was bringing the chalice, cups, and ciboria to him at the altar. The man, who was a little younger than the other new guests, seemed at home in his duties. He had a broad smile and peaceful eyes that seemed to look straight into Father Bernard. He almost appeared *otherworldly*. Hesitating, Father bowed toward the man, then began the Eucharistic Prayer.

Father Bernard approached the server, who came forward right on time with a bowl of water and a towel to purify the priest's hands. Glancing upward toward the crucifix, Father gasped, almost falling down to his knees. The wooden carving of Jesus was not on the cross! It was simply gone! Recovering his senses, he looked to the server in desperation. After bowing to the priest, the man simply smiled and seemed to encourage Father Bernard to continue.

Confused, Father somehow continued with the Eucharistic Prayer, as much out of habit as out of necessity. Adjusting the missal with shaking hands, he began the words that today, all of a sudden, seemed more certain and real.

Facing his *flock*, Father momentarily surveyed the people to see if perhaps, just perhaps, they were also seeing the vacant cross above the altar. Joe and Sister Cecilia's eyes appeared to be transfixed on the empty cross. The mayor and most of the parishioners apparently saw the crucifix as normal with nothing different. They had normal expressions on their faces, expressions of stolid, nonemotional demeanor. However, when Father looked at the visiting strangers in the church, their eyes were riveted not on the cross but on the altar.

Chapter 5

The Eucharistic Celebration

I am the living bread which came down from
heaven: if any man eat of this bread, he shall
live for ever: and the bread that I will give is my
flesh, which I will give for the life of the world

—John 6:51

The priest slowly turned back to the altar and extended his hands over the gifts of bread and wine. At the ringing of the bells, he began the "Epiclesis," a prayer to the Holy Spirit to transform and consecrate the bread and wine into the body and blood of Christ Jesus. The server rang the bells, reminding the congregation of Christ's presence. Father held up the consecrated host as the Body of Christ and the chalice with the Precious Blood of Christ for the congregation to not only see but for an opportunity to join the priest and Christ in offering the sacrifice to God the Father. At that moment, Father Bernard felt the Divine presence growing within him. His face took on a strong peaceful radiance.

Father knew without a doubt that Christ was truly present at that moment with him on the altar and in the Holy Sacrament.

Turning ever so slightly, he saw the young man behind him kneeling in a prayerful manner but with his deep, brown eyes fixed on the Eucharist. With awe and awakening, Fr. Bernard felt profound gratitude at that moment. Taking a deep breath, he willed himself to look upward at the hanging cross and saw the carving of Christ back on the cross, looking down at him as it always had. He slowly regained his composure and extending his hands, led the parish in the Lord's Prayer.

As parishioners were offering the sign of peace to one another, Sister Cecelia, Joe, and Mary Margaret gasped collectively as the figure of Christ seemed to suddenly but quietly *reappear* on the cross above the altar.

Together, the parish said the great penance words of "I am not worthy…but only say the word and my soul will be healed," and then reverently came up to receive Holy Communion. Each person receiving the Eucharist. Father, especially today, felt joined with them and Christ in the Holy Sacrament.

After Father purified the sacred vessels, he took his seat. Taking more time than usual, he quietly reflected on all that had happened this special morning. Today's Mass brought a renewal in his trust and faith in Christ. He knew he was not alone. Completing the final prayers, he dismissed the congregation with "the Mass is ended, go in peace, and be a visible sign of Christ's presence."

Before leaving, he turned toward the parishioners to lead them in prayer, asking St. Michael the Archangel for his special intercession. Father's eyes were drawn toward an unknown, large, imposing man in the last pew who had dark hair and striking eyes. The stranger appeared to be wearing a red cloak. Father bowed toward the tabernacle and then looking back noticed the man was gone.

Chapter 6

After Mass

I am Gabriel, who stand before God. I was sent to speak
to you and to announce to you this good news.

—Luke 1:19

With the parishioners departed, the church assumed a stillness that seemed to suit the occasion. It was empty, with the exception of Sister Cecelia, who sat half-praying, half in awe of what she had seen and experienced. As the sun reached farther into the morning sky, and the church became fully illuminated, a solitary figure entered through the doors and slowly walked up the aisle then sat next to Sister Cecelia.

Joe, watching from the sacristy door, saw Raphael lean forward and tenderly put his arm around the older nun seemingly calming her. After a few moments of conversation, the man put his hands on Sister's head and began praying with her in a deep, peaceful, quiet way.

Suddenly, another one of the *visitors* came over and introduced himself to Joe. He extended his hand and received a warm handshake in return. "What can I do for you, sir?" Joe asked. Smiling, he put his hand on Joe's shoulder, and immediately Joe felt at peace. He even noticed his injured right leg straightening out some. "What a nice church," the stranger remarked. "I thought your pastor gave an inspired homily. Have you heard the saying that the Holy Spirit speaks the language of love?" asked the stranger. Joe agreed that Father's homily that morning had been the best he'd heard, perhaps ever. "By the way Joe, is Father busy? I know that there's a lot to do right after Mass, but I thought he might be able to spare me a few minutes."

Walking without his old discomfort, Joe invited the man back into the sacristy and then went to check with Father

Bernard. The fellow thanked him and settled comfortably onto a wooden stool next to Father's soft, leather chair.

Closing the sacristy door, Joe walked down the hall and knocked on Father's office door. Often Father went directly to his office, right after the Mass, and didn't want to be disturbed. "Yes," came the answer from inside. "Father, there's a visitor in the sacristy who wants to spend a few minutes with you. It seems he's one of those fellas that was at Mass this morning. Says his name is Gabriel!" Joe, realizing that the name of the stranger had just come to him, and he hadn't even asked for the man's name, decided that the name just seemed to fit. Hesitantly, Father replied, "Tell him I'll be down in a minute."

Immediately following the Mass, Fr. Bernard had gone to his office and hung up his Lenten vestments. Not sure of what he had experienced and encountered, he sat down and tried to slow down his heart and pray for an answer. He asked himself what had happened to the crucifix. Yet he was sure the *real presence* of Jesus had been with him at the altar. *Those strangers who appeared suddenly in the church serving and reading the scriptures, where had they come from? Who were they*, he asked himself. How could all this be happening in his church, in the far reaches of Missouri? What did it all mean? And now a man named Gabriel waiting to see him! Father Bernard knew very well that Gabriel was the name given to God's angel messenger, the one who had two thousand years ago announced to the Virgin Mary that she would be the mother of the Messiah. Yet a man named Gabriel was waiting for him in the sacristy! It was all too much, too soon, and too astounding to believe. Wondering what God was telling him, he reflected and slowly began to *see* and *grasp* what was actually happening in his parish, to his parishioners, and to himself.

Summoning all his courage, Father got up and walked toward the sacristy, with his right hand grasping the Holy Rosary he kept in his pocket. It was to be the most eventful walk of his life.

After Father Bernard opened the door, Gabriel was the first to speak. "Don't be afraid, Father," Gabriel said in a quiet but steady voice.

"Afraid of what?" the priest replied, in a voice that quivered with anticipation and nervousness.

"Afraid of what just happened and most importantly what will happen," Gabriel answered.

Father Bernard slowly raised his eyes and looked at Gabriel who projected a calm expression and posture. "What's going to happen? What do you mean?" he asked.

Leaning forward in his chair, Gabriel looked directly into the questioning eyes of Father Bernard. He reached out and took the priest's right hand in his. With a firm, but gentle squeeze, he said, "I came to give you a message."

Surprised, Father withdrew his hand but continued to stare at Gabriel with eyebrows raised, not saying anything.

Gabriel continued, "Our Lord understands your struggles with your priestly vocation, your calling. He knows your heart. It's no coincidence that you were assigned to St. Thomas the

Apostle Parish. Remember St. Thomas was the Apostle with doubts? Jesus desires to assure you that His love and His presence are truly here with you during Mass, and He is always with you. He will never forsake you." Gabriel continued, "Sometimes our Lord invites us in new ways to trust Him. Doubt is part of the human condition, and priests are not immune from questioning their vocation. But faith and obedience to Christ always break through and become a bridge. Christ has specially called you to serve and shepherd the people of St. Thomas Parish. The Holy Spirit is always here to help answer your questions, soften your angst, and guide you closer to the truth, the message of the cross."

Patiently reminding Father Bernard, Gabriel continued, "St. Thomas Church is not just a building in need of repair but folks searching for communion with Christ and in community with each other. As you know, the church is the body of Christ and is to be shared by all and requires not only your leadership but also your listening and trust in others."

Gabriel's voice became stronger, "So, Father Bernard, trust in what you are doing here at this parish, at this time, with the people of God. That's the message I bring to you today. Two thousand years ago in Nazareth, young Mary, the mother of our Lord, also questioned. Yet her trust in God, her yes, still lights the way."

Father Bernard sat in silence with his mouth open, unable to speak, trying to take all this encounter in.

Gabriel rose and moving to the door gave Father a slight bow of his head and silently left. Father Bernard just sat there, rubbing his eyes to make sure he wasn't dreaming. A serene feeling came over him. Rising, he went out into the church, coming to rest on one of the pews so recently polished and oiled by Joe earlier in the morning. It had been quite a morning!

Feeling more at peace, he felt grateful that he had been called and sent to serve this community of believers. Father had new insights and hope for his *flock* (and himself).

Lifting his eyes up toward the crucifix with nervous anticipation, he again saw the familiar figure of Jesus on the cross, with arms outstretched and head bent toward him. As the afternoon sun continued its journey to the west, its beams cast shadows over the sanctuary and especially the crucified figure of Jesus.

The church was empty. Not a single sound came from within, just a special stillness that was filling the church. His hands came to rest on the back of the pew in front of him, and for some time, apparently longer than he realized, he just knelt there. Christ's love and peace entered his heart, where before fear and angst had dwelt.

Chapter 7

Evening Comes

Did I not tell you that if you believe
you will see the glory of God?

—John 11:40

It was about 4:00 p.m. when Joe reentered the church, and looking up at the crucifix, he felt a sense of normalcy return. He noticed Father Bernard kneeling in the pew but decided not to interrupt him, as he seemed in deep contemplation.

And who wouldn't be? Joe thought. After the events of this morning, with the figure of Christ missing from the cross and later reappearing, the collection of assorted strangers at the church service, and the various visitors to the sacristy. Who wouldn't be lost in contemplation? It had been a strange and somewhat disconcerting day, but now the church seemed at peace in the twilight of the winter day. The shadows played over the pews and sanctuary as the sun continued its journey over the church shining through the western windows.

Continuing along the rear of the main hall, Joe stopped by the old confessional where he had found the sleeping fellow earlier in the day. Checking inside to assure himself that the man had not sneaked back in to spend another night, he found on the floor of the confessional a small, battered leather bag. Picking it up, he opened the pouch, and many small unfamiliar coins spilled out. They seemed to have the likeness of a king on one side. Putting the coins back into the pouch, he placed it in his pocket, and he continued on across the back of the church and into the narthex. He checked each bathroom and the coat room for signs of vagrants. All seemed normal, a normal ending to an abnormal day.

Since there was no event scheduled in the parish this evening (which was unusual), Joe began to close up the church. As he made his familiar rounds, he noticed a light shining through the partially open door of the sacristy. He slowly walked to the door, and seeing the priest sitting in the leather chair, knocked softly.

"Father, need anything before I finish locking up and go?"

"No thanks, Joe," Father Bernard replied kindly. Joe paused, somewhat startled that Fr. Bernard had not called him by his more formal name. *Perhaps*, Joe thought, *this was the beginning of a new relationship.* Smiling, he hoped that Father would start being friendly with Sam, his dog.

As he turned to leave, he remembered the coins. "Father, I found these coins in a pouch in the confessional where that fellow Raphael was sleeping. Don't know what they are, but I thought you might know." He handed the pouch to the pastor and silently left the sacristy heading home with Sam.

The priest held the pouch in his hands for some time, noticing that the leather was well-worn, even dusty. He then spilled out the coins on the end table near his chair and slowly turned each one over in his right hand. Recognizing the image of Caesar, it occurred to him to send them over to the University at Rolla. His friend was a professor there specializing in ancient history and Israel. Placing the coins back into the pouch and into his desk drawer, he rose, turned out the light, and locked the sacristy door. Glancing again up at the crucifix, he genuflected then walked slowly toward the door to the rectory.

Postscript

Commit your way to the Lord:
trust that God will act.

—Psalm 37:5

It was two weeks before Father Bernard received the letter from his friend at the university, concerning the coins he had sent him for evaluation.

The professor was excited. The letter said that most of the coins were Roman coins from the first century, called *dinars*, the standard coin of exchange in the Roman Empire at the time of Christ. Some were made of silver and gold. He suggested that they were of substantially more value. The professor validated their authenticity and indicated that the university museum or other noteworthy museums would be very interested in the collection. He estimated their net worth at about $200,000. Some were apparently very rare.

As Father Bernard sat back into his leather chair, he mulled over what it all could possibly mean. It took some time to take it all in. Questions about what he had experienced still remained, but his friend's letter proposed to Father evidence that the coins had been purposefully delivered to St. Thomas Parish by one of Jesus's messengers.

Later that day, Father Bernard eagerly called the new president of the parish council. "Ralph, let's have a meeting of the council this coming week. Something has come up, which might mean that our plans to do that needed maintenance on the church will be possible. Perhaps we could even open up a daycare center for poor families right here on the parish grounds."

Excited, Father felt a new opportunity to go beyond the walls of the church and bring Christ more into the community. He had even been considering the pouring of a basketball court for the young folks to help them feel a part of the parish. Those memories of good times playing ball at the seminary always gave him a lift.

He hoped those layoffs of church personnel might not be needed now. He especially would be grateful for Sister Cecelia staying. Her wisdom and support of the families was a treasure to the parish.

After sharing the good news with Ralph, Father Bernard got up and walked into the main church. Still in awe of the recent events, he was grateful for this renewal of joy and hope about to be celebrated on the upcoming Easter morning. Sitting on one of the aging pews, and gazing up at the crucifix, he prayed, "Lord, I thank you for believing in me and loving me. Thank you for your daily presence in our lives at St. Thomas. Help us to take your message to others."

Looking up at the figure of Christ on the cross and as the evening shadows cast new highlights across the sanctuary, Father Bernard imagined he saw a slight smile on his Savior's face and a flicker from the red votive candle.

Listing of Characters in Order of Appearance

Joe—Long-time custodian at St. Thomas Parish in Jasper, Missouri. It was he who first recognizes the figure of Jesus is *missing* from the cross above the altar. A *believer*, he introduces the *messengers* to Father Bernard and is among the first to *see* Christ's figure reappear on the cross during the Mass.

Sam—Joe's service dog. Apparently, Joe was wounded in Vietnam and his black lab service dog is his best friend, a stable presence during a time of turmoil.

Raphael—One of God's three sainted archangels, his name means *healer*. He is known for leading those struggling, bringing them closer to God. He is thus the patron saint of travelers and always has a *staff* with him. He is the first *messenger* to appear at the parish.

Father Bernard—Pastor of St. Thomas Parish. Unsatisfied with his assignment questioning why he was not given a more academic posting by his Bishop. Introverted and often controlling, now questioning his *call* to the priesthood.

Mayor Miller—Long-time resident of the city and parish, going through a divorce after a long marriage; looking forward to moving away from his situation. Is he a Catholic in name only?

Diane and Daughter Kathleen—Young, a single mother concerned about providing for her young disfigured daughter, who is one of the first to recognize that Jesus's figure is not on the cross.

Martha—Friendly, dedicated parishioner and morning Mass attendee. Her faith is expressed in a ministry of service and hospitality.

Mary Margaret—Martha's younger sister. Diagnosed with cancer, and she has a husband with dementia. Her faith is expressed in a deep devotion to prayer and reflection.

Sister Cecilia—Only nun in the parish; recently relieved of her duties as religious educator by Fr. Bernard. Concerned about reassignment to another parish or even retirement. She feels sadness at possibly leaving her beloved parish families.

The server—One of the *visitors* to the parish that morning; a companion of Raphael. Is he one of the younger apostles? Or who?

St. Michael, the Archangel—The man with the red cloak, sitting at the rear of the church during Mass. He is the highest angel, leading God's *army*. A late and unobtrusive visitor to the parish. Known for being a guardian of others.

Gabriel—The second of the angels to visit Father Bernard. He was God's messenger to the Virgin Mary. Gabriel *brings* God's love, reassurance, and peace to the pastor.

The professor—Fr. Bernard's university friend who verifies the authenticity of the coins left in the confessional by Raphael, as original Roman coins from the First Century.

Ralph—New president of the parish council; he receives an unexpected call from Fr. Bernard that the parish has come into some funds, which will allow several unfunded projects to begin.

....

Behold, I am sending my messenger ahead
of you; he will prepare your way.

—Mark 1:2

Simply I learned about her, and
ungrudgingly do I share—her riches
I do not hide away; For to men she
is an unfailing treasure; those who
gain this treasure win the friendship
of God, to whom the gifts they have
from discipline commend them.

—Solomon speaking about Wisdom
Wisdom 7:13–14

Some years ago as my dad was coming out of surgery, he aspirated. He was put into an induced coma on a ventilator to allow his lungs to heal. By the time I got there from Washington, D.C., he was still in a coma. Dad never recovered. For over a week, he hovered between life and death, and I was simply depressed, drinking more than I should. I decided that if he miraculously recovered, I would move him from Florida to my home in Arizona. I further decided to take all the furniture and his things and move it to storage. Later I could ship all these to our home in Arizona when he recovered. I rented a storage unit and a moving truck and parked them in front of Dad's house. Not being of sound mind nor body at that time, I suddenly realized that I couldn't move all that stuff into storage by myself, and I had no help in the town.

As I became more and more downtrodden, the doorbell rang. A young man I had never seen was at the door. He said he had been a music student of my dad's, who had retired. He said that he heard that my dad was sick (I hadn't let that news out), and he decided to come by and see if he could help. Grateful for his help, we spent the day loading furniture and stuff into the truck and taking it over to a storage unit. It took us all day. Thanking the young man, I told him I'd let him know about my dad. Then later, I realized I didn't have his number. I never saw him again. I can't remember his name but will never forget his presence in my life that day and how he just showed up.

Later in life, I came to realize that God's messengers are real! I am convinced to this day that the young man at my door was sent from God to help me when I needed it most in my hour of darkness. It was no accident that he showed up and offered to help.

In my diaconate formation and over a decade of service to the Church, I have come to believe that God is truly nearer than I first thought. Our *helpers* (God's messengers) may not be as visible or identifiable as Gabriel or Raphael in this story. Nevertheless, they come and go in and out of our lives. We just need to be awake and aware of these sacred encounters. Remember, Mary's husband, Joseph, acted three times on the words of an angel who came to him in a dream.

In the middle of the COVID pandemic, as a Deacon in the Roman Catholic Church, I was blessed to be able to offer First Holy Communion to two of my grandchildren. (At the time, the Mass had to be outside for safety reasons.) That day, I realized that after an army career of thirty-five years perhaps, this was one of the reasons I was ordained a deacon…to baptize and then bring them Christ in the sacrament of Holy Communion. You see, we really may not know the true and sacred purpose of our lives until later in our journey. Walking or sometimes running through our life often doesn't allow us to stop, reflect, and readjust.

Perhaps we are put here on earth for many different interactions and encounters, some of which we may think are small and insignificant. Yet to the person we help or befriend, it could be one of the most significant events in *their* lives.

I've come to realize how interconnected our lives really are, and how the threads of our "events" are woven with others' experiences. Often, I wonder why my wife and I have moved so often from one place or parish to another. Yet I try to gratefully reflect on these journeys as opportunities to learn and share with others. Nature too is intertwined with our lives and those of others. It's only now in my mid-seventies that life becomes a little clearer, a little more *real*, and I begin to see my part in it.

We are not walking this life alone. God is with us. Family, friends, and many others bless us on our journey. Open your door. He will walk right in.

There's a great song, written by Mary Gauthier, one of our favorite writers of life, called "Walking Each Other Home."

For over fifty years, we are still walking each other home.

Peace, Deacon John, Lenten Season 2022

1. What character do you personally identify with in this story?

2. Recall when Christ has sent unexpected messengers into your life. Did you recognize them? Who were they?

3. Where are you on your faith journey? As you look backward at your life, what events changed your life and led you to Christ? Were these encounters just coincidences or perhaps *Christ-incidences*?

4. In your daily life, when are your close moments and encounters with Christ? Do I let my fears/doubts keep me from seeing God's presence?

5. Our story has tried to include the seven sacraments. Can you identify them?

6. The cross is where God truly reveals His great love for us. We chose to make the crucifix a focus of his story. It has been written that there is "no Easter without the cross." What of your own experiences helps you understand that?